Date: 3/28/17

J 006.7 ANN
Anniss, Matt,
Create your own podcast /

Media Genius

CREATE YOUR OWN

PODCAST

Matt Anniss

CAPSTONE PRESS
a capstone imprint

Edited by James Benefield and Helen Cox Cannons
Designed by Steve Mead
Original illustrations © Capstone Global Library 2016
Picture research by Morgan Walters
Production by Victoria Fitzgerald
Originated by Capstone Global Library
Printed and bound in China

20 19 18 17 16
10 9 8 7 6 5 4 3 2 1

Library of Congress Cataloging-in-Publication Data
Cataloging-in-publication data is available at the Library of Congress.
ISBN 978-1-4109-8109-7 (hardback)
ISBN 978-1-4109-8113-4 (ebook PDF)

Acknowledgments
The author and publisher are grateful to the following for permission to reproduce copyright
material: Alamy: Daily Mail/Rex, 6; Getty Images: David M. Benett, 41, Inti St Clair, 42, Johnny
Nunez, 10, Kirk McKoy, 43, Marc Romanelli, 40, Rubberball/Mark Andersen, 38; iStockphoto:
Chris Schmidt, 36, digitalskillet, 14, xijian, cover, 4; Jordan Agolli, 5; Newscom: Michael Melia/
Retna Pictures/ZUMAPRESS, 39, Sam Simmonds/Polaris, 16; Shutterstock: AnastasiaN,
(globe) top 4, Antonio Guillem, 33, Carlos E. Santa Maria, 15, Di Studio, 13, Edyta Pawlowska,
34, Ellica, 7, Everett Collection, 8, gabriel12, 28, gasa, 24, Helga Esteb, 20, Iaremenko Sergii,
bottom 22, Ingvar Bjork, bottom 23, jocic, top 22, kak2s, bottom 19, maxik, 17, Maya
Kruchankova, 21, Nata-Lia, top 23, Nejron Photo, 11, Nomad_Soul, 32, PathDoc, 25, R-studio,
design element throughout, SkillUp, 26-27, stock_shot, 30, wavebreakmedia, 29, 31, zentilia,
middle 23; Teri Pengilley, 39; Wikimedia: varnent, 37

We would like to thank Neil Denny and Helen Zaltzmann for their invaluable help in the
preparation of this book.

Every effort has been made to contact copyright holders of material reproduced in this book.
Any omissions will be rectified in subsequent printings if notice is given to the publisher.

PO007590LEOF16

Table of Contents

Broadcasting to the World!

Have you ever wanted to host your own radio show? Do you have a hobby that you're passionate about, or a desire to talk enthusiastically about your favorite subjects? Maybe you just like the idea of spending time with friends, talking with classmates, or making people laugh? Podcasts are a great way to do all of these things and make a really interesting program, too!

You don't have to be a radio star to host your own radio show. Now you can do it yourself, thanks to the wonderful world of podcasting!

Podcasts and podcasters

A podcast is a bit like a radio show, but it can be about any subject or be any length. Also, instead of being broadcast on the radio, it's stored on the Internet and can be streamed and downloaded. This means people can listen to podcasts whenever they feel like it. "Podcaster" is the name given to people who create and publish podcasts.

21st-century radio

Many popular radio shows, such as *This American Life*, are also successfully released as podcasts after broadcast. Yet most podcasters are just enthusiastic members of the public with no formal links to radio stations. Podcasters don't need links with radio stations, since creating podcasts is really easy to do.

Success Story

Jordan Agolli, a 19-year-old from Georgia, USA, started his own podcast after he recognized teenagers needed more support in their entrepreneurial journey. Jordan started his first business at 14 years old and wished he had more support and guidance at that age. In March 2014, he launched Teenage Entrepreneur, which quickly became a success. Jordan now has nearly 3,000 followers on Facebook and listeners in 68 countries.

CHAPTER 1

Podcasts for
BEGINNERS

Although podcasting isn't a new idea, it's still quite a young art form. The word "podcasting" dates back to 2004. In 2004, former MTV host Adam Curry developed a software program called iPodder for downloading and storing Internet radio shows. The word "podcast" referred to Apple's popular portable MP3 player, the iPod, and is said to have been coined by journalist Ben Hammersley.

Listening to podcasts is a very popular pastime—and it is getting more popular all the time. In 2014, 15 percent of American adults said they'd listened to a podcast in the past month.

The popularity of podcasting was fueled by the iPod. However, podcasts can be downloaded and played on all computers, portable music players, and mobile devices. Today, you don't even need to download podcasts. You can stream podcasts on web sites such as SoundCloud and Mixcloud.

Podcast world

Whether you use iTunes or not, it's never been easier to find and listen to podcasts. Podcasts are everywhere, so it's easy to find them. They can be found in so many places because they can be about all kinds of subjects. Podcasts can be about absolutely anything you want, whether serious, silly, or somewhere in between.

THE KNOWLEDGE

The most popular place to find podcasts is Apple's iTunes Store. In 2013, Apple announced that the store featured over 250,000 podcast series plus 8 million individual episodes, in more than 100 languages. The company also expected podcast subscriptions—where listeners sign up for automatic downloads of new episodes—to top 1 billion in 2014!

Different strokes for different folks

Podcasters don't need to persuade the bosses of radio stations to give them a show. They are free to pursue their own interests and develop their own ideas, and they don't always seek a big audience. This means that there are podcasts about almost every subject you can think of, each with their own individual style.

In the early days of radio, there was very little choice for listeners. Podcasts allow listeners to find shows and episodes that match their interests, and to listen at a time that fits their schedule.

There are a number of different show formats used by podcasters. These include:

- **monologues,** where one person gives his or her opinion or talks about a subject

- **panel discussions,** where a number of people discuss topics with a host

- **magazine-style shows,** featuring a mix of reporting by different people with their own styles

- **documentaries,** where one story is covered in detail, often using interviews

- **drama,** where one or more person acts out a story.

Take football as an example. In addition to podcasts about different teams, you'll also find series focused on fantasy football, football video games, and discussions about hot topics within the sport. While radio stations are often required to provide balanced coverage, podcasters aren't. You could make a podcast just about your team.

Choose your subject

Browse a list of the world's most popular podcasts, and you'll find that many different topics and styles are represented. These include:

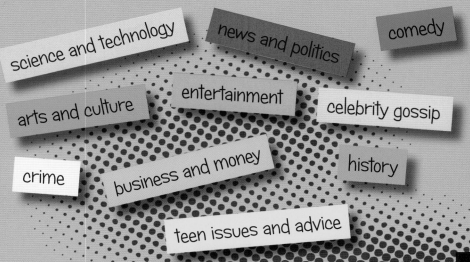

science and technology

news and politics

comedy

entertainment

arts and culture

celebrity gossip

crime

business and money

history

teen issues and advice

Music makes the world go round

Many of the world's most popular podcasts are focused on music. Some music podcasts are downloadable versions of traditional radio shows, while others showcase DJ mixes or simply focus on a particular style of music. One of the world's most downloaded podcasts is NPR.org's *All Songs Considered*. This podcast picks out the best new releases from across the musical spectrum.

Pro Tip

Many podcasters are able to play music in their shows because they pay for the privilege. In the United States, licenses to play music on podcasts can be purchased from ASCAP (the American Society of Composers, Authors, and Publishers). Licenses are not cheap, partly because they are mostly aimed at professionals, web site owners, and media organizations.

Like many of the world's top DJs, Tiësto records his own podcasts. On his podcasts, fans can listen to him mixing tracks whenever they like.

If you get permission, you can record a performance from an unsigned local band (one that hasn't signed a contract with a record company) and use it in your podcast.

Legal issues

Most music, and certainly all the songs you've heard on the radio, is covered by copyright. That means somebody owns the music, and you cannot play it in a podcast unless you have permission. However, not all music is covered by copyright. Many podcasters use music that's been created to use for free, under certain conditions. This kind of music can be found on web sites such as the Free Music Archive or paid-for services such as Melody Loops.

What's the recipe for success?

Different podcasts are successful for different reasons. Some appeal to a certain type of person, or listeners with very specific interests. So what makes the best podcasts so good? Are there any similarities between the world's greatest podcasts? To find out, listen to several podcasts on your favorite topics and review what you hear. You can find podcasts arranged by category in the iTunes Store, as well as charts of popular series.

How to review podcasts

Before you start, try to find three or four podcasts that cover a subject you're interested in. This way, you can compare and contrast styles, features, and approaches of different podcasts. Then, sit down with a pen and paper, listen to each podcast, and write down your answers to the following questions for each of them:

- How long is the podcast? How often do new episodes appear?

- What format does it follow? (Think about the number of hosts, whether there are guests, how they use music and sound effects, and anything else you think is relevant.)

- What topics does the podcast cover? How much time is spent covering each topic?

- How is the podcast presented by the host or the hosts? For example, is the podcast serious, laidback, chatty, or funny?

- What do you like or not like about it?

Once you've reviewed each podcast, take a look at your notes. Can you see any patterns developing, such as recurring themes, similar features, or successful presentational styles? Bear in mind that with podcasts you can also do something that can't be found anywhere else.

If you're going to make a great podcast, you need to figure out what makes the most popular series so successful. What is it about them that people like so much?

CHAPTER 2

Planning Your PODCAST

By now, you should have a good idea about what podcast styles you enjoy. You might have even thought about the subjects that you'd like to cover. That's a good start, but there's a lot more planning to do before you can sit down to record your first podcast episode.

Even the most fluid-sounding podcasts are usually the result of lots of very careful planning.

Themes, angles, and hooks

The first stage in the process is to settle on a theme or angle for your podcast. Start by choosing a theme that can be used again and again. Then decide on the way you'll approach it. If you get the theme right, listeners will be more likely to stick with the podcast over a number of episodes. They can become subscribers on iTunes, then listen on their phone, MP3 player, or computer. You can also listen to podcasts on streaming services such as SoundCloud and Mixcloud.

Once you've figured out your theme and angle, why not consider what hooks you might use to entice would-be listeners? A hook is a way to present the information. For example, if you chose cooking as a theme, your angle might be hilarious mistakes made in the kitchen. Your hook could then be featuring a different cook in each episode, who describes his or her mistakes before explaining how you can avoid them.

Success Story

To create a successful podcast, you don't have to focus on the same subject for every episode. *The Stuff You Should Know* podcast focuses on a different subject in each episode. This approach has proved extremely popular. In total, its episodes have been downloaded more than 100 million times on iTunes.

"Content is king!"

A theme, angle, and hook will encourage listeners to check out your podcast. But to turn people into dedicated subscribers, you need to make sure the content is top notch.

The content in your podcast depends on your theme, angle, and the subject. Are you covering a popular subject, such as television? If so, you'll need to think very carefully about style and content. It's especially important to stand out when there is a lot of competition.

If your subject is more obscure, it's less likely to have been covered by many other people. Podcasts with obscure subjects might not get millions of listeners, but there could be a smaller, but very interested, audience just waiting for a podcast on the topic. Whatever path you choose, coming up with fresh, interesting content is very important.

Some popular podcasts blend fact, opinion, and jokes. On their hit podcast *Radiolab*, co-hosts Robert Krulwich and Jad Abumrad include scientific facts but also funny banter with expert guests.

When conducting research, find reliable sources for the information you'll be presenting. There are two types of sources: primary and secondary sources. Primary sources are documents or original objects written or created during the period you're researching, such as diaries, news footage, interviews, clothing, and buildings. Secondary sources are those written or created later that discuss the period you're researching. These sources range from history books and magazine articles to modern documentaries about the subject.

When coming up with content for your podcasts, it's important to do lots of research. Packing your podcasts with facts—especially those checked with at least two sources—will lend weight to your episodes.

Structuring your podcast

Some podcasters like to "freestyle" during recordings. This involves coming up with things to say and topics to cover on the spot. Other podcasters prefer to have a plan. They come up with a basic framework for their episodes, which can then be changed around as they get more comfortable with the recording process. For example, if you were making a magazine-style radio show, you'd come up with a list of regular features or topics for discussion. Some of these topics might appear in the same place from show to show. These can then be arranged into features of different lengths, depending on the content.

Organizing your ideas

You don't need to get things right with your first podcast, but you might still find it useful to come up with a plan. You can then figure out how long you might spend on each segment, feature, or discussion. This outline can then be turned into a rough working script, featuring suggestions for things to say between segments (known as links). To get you started, here's an example of a podcast plan for a magazine show.

SCHOOL LIFE PODCAST

Total length: 20 minutes

INTRODUCTION

DAVE: Hello, I'm Dave.

SALLY: And I'm Sally.

DAVE: Welcome to the first episode of the *School Life* podcast!

SALLY: We're going to start the show by discussing what's hot and what's not at school this week!

SEGMENT 1: WHAT'S HOT AND WHAT'S NOT

(5 minutes)

LINK

DAVE: Next, we're going to introduce you to one of the newest teachers at school, Mr. Smith. After math class, Sally went to interview him.

SEGMENT 2: MR. SMITH INTERVIEW
(5 minutes, recorded)

LINK
DAVE: Thanks, Sally. Now it's time to talk school sports with hockey captain, Tina, and Christian, who's the football team's star quarterback.

SEGMENT 3: SCHOOL SPORTS DISCUSSION
(6 minutes)

LINK
SALLY: Thanks to Tina and Christian for joining us. Now Dave has news about this year's school play.

SEGMENT 4: SCHOOL PLAY REPORT
(4 minutes, recorded)

OUTRO
SALLY: That's all we have time for this week. If you've liked what you've heard, don't forget to subscribe to get future episodes.
DAVE: Yes, and you can also follow us on social media to get updates between episodes...

Style and tone

Great content is just one important ingredient of the world's best podcasts. Try listening to a mixture of well-known podcasts. You'll soon find that the best always feature hosts who have their own unique voice. In this case, "voice" doesn't mean what they sound like, but rather how they conduct themselves on the microphone. Some are laidback and chatty, while others are very serious. All seem comfortable in front of the microphone, creating an on-air experience that makes listeners want to hear more.

Finding your voice

The style you use sets the tone of the podcast. It should be appropriate to the content of your show, but should also come naturally. If your podcast investigates serious topics, it might be inappropriate to crack jokes. If being serious doesn't come naturally to you, there's no point forcing yourself to act this way.

Successful podcasters, such as Chris Hardwick, have their own style. On average, Hardwick's *Nerdist* podcast is downloaded nearly 5 million times a month.

So, if your podcast is going to be a success, you need to find your voice. It's a chance to show off your personality. Whether you're passionate and knowledgeable, or playful and silly, listeners will respond if it comes from the heart. Why not try experimenting with different presentational styles until you find one that you're comfortable with?

THE KNOWLEDGE

In 2011, podcaster Sally Hille set a new world record. She was 94 years old when she was officially crowned the World's Oldest DJ! At the time, she recorded a weekly podcast from her home in Marietta, Ohio.

You don't need to get the recording of your first podcast right the first time. You could record a number of versions in different styles, then decide on the one you like best.

CHAPTER 3

Making Your

PODCAST

THE PERFECT PODCASTING SET-UP

Portable voice recorder

Many smartphones can be used to record interviews, using free-to-download applications ("apps" for short). You can also buy a portable voice recorder. This contains a built-in mic to record interviews. Recordings are stored on the device and can later be copied to a computer.

Microphone and stand

Look for a mic that connects to a computer using a USB cable. This way, you will not need to buy any extra equipment, such as a mixing desk or sound card. The mic should be on a stand, on a steady table, to help get cleaner, crisper recordings.

Now that you're ready with a rough plan, a unique vision, and a head full of ideas, you're just about ready to make your first podcast. Before you can dive in, though, you'll need equipment to record your episodes.

Equipment options

Exactly what equipment you'll need depends on the type of show you'll be making. If you plan to record interviews with people on the go—for example, at school or in a local community center—then you'll need a portable device. If you're planning to record the show in one place, you might only need a computer, microphone ("mic" for short), and a pair of headphones.

Headphones
You need headphones to listen to the recording and monitor sound levels before you press the "record" button.

Computer
Use a computer to record your podcast, edit it afterward, and then share it with the world. Some podcasters also record their interviews and panel discussions using free computer-to-computer call software, such as Skype, Ringr, or Viber.

External storage device
You can use this to store your high-quality audio recordings. They are useful because podcast recordings can take up a lot of space on a computer's internal hard drive.

Recording your podcast

It's natural to be nervous about recording, but try to have fun! It's your chance to get on the mic, so talk about the things you're passionate about and create something you're proud of.

Before you begin, check that you have everything in place for the recording. You're probably using a computer to do this. This is something the vast majority of podcasters do. If so, you'll need to plug in the mic and then download some recording software.

Pro Tip

Some computers come with recording software built in, such as GarageBand on Apple computers. If your computer doesn't have this, download some free software, such as Audacity. When you make the podcast, be sure the software is set to record in a high-quality audio format, such as AIFF or WAV. This will ensure better-sounding podcasts.

The big day has finally arrived, and you're ready to record your first podcast. Enjoy the experience, and don't stress out if things go wrong—very few people get it right the first time!

Don't worry if you make mistakes or the recording takes longer than you think. You can cut out parts you don't like or trim your podcast down to the right length during the editing process.

The recording process

There are many different ways to record a podcast. You can:

- do it at home or school, recording the entire episode in one try
- record a number of reports or features in different locations, either using your computer or a portable recorder (such as a cell phone). You can edit it together afterward.
- record it at home, in stages, over a number of days or weeks.

Before you start, read through any scripts you have or notes you've taken. Also, do a quick test to see how you sound. If the test recording sounds fuzzy and distorted, that means your mouth was too close to the mic. If it's too quiet, you need to move closer to the mic.

Editing your podcast

Even if you've captured a great recording, editing can still be used to improve the quality of your show. Editing is the process of selecting, sequencing, and rearranging something. In the case of audio recordings, this is done using editing software. The good news is that you don't always need any extra programs—sometimes you can edit your podcast using the same software with which you recorded it. If you have recorded on your phone or a recorder, you may need to transfer the files to your computer before opening them in an editing software app.

Understanding the editing screen
Exact features vary from app to app, but all popular editing programs share similar features. Here are some of them:

1. WAVEFORM

This is a way of showing what you've just recorded, on-screen. If you use the zoom tool to get a better look, you'll notice that it rises and falls, just like a wave. The tallest parts of the wave are the loudest sections of the recording, with quieter parts represented by shorter waves.

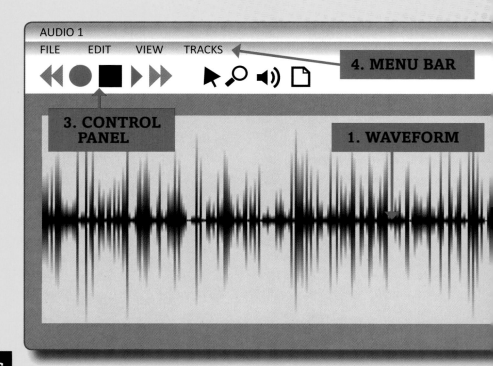

AUDIO 1

FILE   EDIT   VIEW   TRACKS

4. MENU BAR

3. CONTROL PANEL

1. WAVEFORM

2. SELECTED AUDIO

Editing software allows you to highlight a section of your recording, either to play it on its own, copy it, or cut it out of the recording file altogether. Once you've highlighted and copied a section of audio, it can then be moved to a different part of the recording.

3. CONTROL PANEL

Here, you'll find buttons representing the main controls you'll need during the editing process. Controls include play, pause, magnify, loop (if you want to listen to a section over and over again), and volume.

4. MENU BAR

Here, you'll find drop-down menus containing lots of other controls. These usually include options to save your project, export it as an MP3 file (when you've finished), and add special effects. There's usually also a help menu, where you'll find answers to frequently asked questions.

Pro Tip

Here are some points to remember when you're working on a computer:

- Always save copies of your unedited work, just in case!
- Use a large external hard drive to store large files, or your computer might slow down.
- Back up files constantly!

← **2. SELECTED AUDIO**

Finishing touches

The good thing about using recording and editing software is that it allows you to layer up sounds, using a process called multitracking. This involves adding extra sound recordings, or tracks, to the file containing your podcast recording. In theory, you can have as many tracks as you want in your recordings. However, including too many tracks might make your podcast sound cluttered and confusing. You can adjust the sound levels in each track using a process called mixing.

During the final stage of editing your podcast, why not add some extra special touches by making your own radio-style jingles? Or perhaps you can ask some musician friends to help you record a theme song.

That's a wrap!

Once you're happy with the sound mix, you're almost done. Before you can share it, you'll need to:

- save it as an MP3 file
- think of a name for the podcast series that nobody else is currently using
- create a logo for the podcast series. Companies, such as iTunes, request the logo to be square (1,400 pixels by 1,400 pixels). It also needs to look good as a small thumbnail-sized picture. Take a look at the logos of popular podcasts on iTunes for ideas.

Pro Tip

Mixing is the process of preparing a music clip or podcast recording for broadcast. During the mixing process, you can alter the sound levels of each separate track, making some things louder and other elements quieter. Mixing can be used to:

- create atmosphere by adding sound effects
- put royalty-free music underneath speech or between segments (although you may have to pay a one-time fee for this)
- break up your podcasts using radio-style jingles.

In professional recording studios, sound engineers use a mixing desk to complete final mixes. Today, you can get similar results using recording and editing software.

CHAPTER 4

Sharing Your
PODCAST

One of the reasons behind the growing popularity of podcasts is that they are easy to access. By using the Internet to distribute episodes, podcasters can reach a global audience. This was something that was close to impossible in the days before the Internet.

You, too, can potentially reach a global audience with your podcast. To do that, you'll need to find a place to store, or host, MP3 files of your episodes.

Pro Tip

Many podcasters choose to launch their own web site to provide fans and would-be listeners with information about their shows. The most important function of a web site is to tell a visitor what the podcast is and how to get it. You can start a new web page for each episode, and gather links to stream and download shows in one place. You can even add lots of other interesting stuff, such as photos and links to other web sites.

By placing your podcast on the Internet, listeners will be able to tune in wherever they are in the world. They could even listen while on the move using mobile devices.

Online options

There are a number of ways to get your podcast on the Internet, but below are the two most popular methods:

1. Upload it to an audio-on-demand web site
These are web sites, such as SoundCloud and Mixcloud, that allow users to upload podcasts and share them. Each user (for example, a podcaster) will have a profile page where listeners will find his or her podcasts, DJ mixes, or radio shows. Fans can listen over the Internet, known as streaming, or download shows to their computer or mobile device.

2. Sign up to a podcast hosting service
These are web sites that host and distribute podcasts. Popular examples include Libsyn, PodOMatic, and Blubrry. Some of these services charge a small monthly fee, though.

The School Life Podcast

ABOUT

Welcome to the School Life Podcast web site! You can find out more about the series by clicking on the "about" link. Click on the audio player to listen to our latest episode, or click on "episodes" to check out previous shows. We're always looking for new contributors, so don't hesitate to contact us if you want to get involved!

ABOUT
EPISODES
CONTACT
LINKS

Latest Episode

Feed me now!

Once you've found somewhere online to store your podcast, you'll also need to create something called an RSS feed. "RSS" is short for either "Rich Site Summary" or "Really Simple Syndication." It is a way of automatically sending out information on the Internet and alerting people it is there. RSS is used by news web sites as well as podcasters.

RSS feeds tell podcast directories such as iTunes what your podcast is all about, and where to find it on the Internet.

The importance of RSS

It's the RSS feed of your podcast that tells subscribers when new episodes have been uploaded. It's possible to create your own RSS feeds (you can find detailed instructions on how to do this online). Podcast-hosting services, such as Libsyn, will do it for you. Your RSS feed will automatically add new episodes of your podcast to directories. This is important, as podcast directories are where most listeners discover new shows.

Get in the directories

There are lots of podcast directories on the Internet, such as Stitcher. Each podcast-hosting service also has its own directory. The most-used podcast directory of all is Apple's iTunes. If you want your podcast to reach a big audience, you'll need to be listed on iTunes.

Pro Tip

Once your podcast has an RSS feed, you can get into the iTunes podcast directory. You can find detailed instructions on how to submit your podcast on the Apple web site. If your podcast is accepted (the vast majority are), then you'll receive a confirmation e-mail. It can take up to two weeks for Apple to approve a new podcast, so make sure you wait until you have that confirmation before telling the world!

Many listeners recommend their favorite podcasts to friends. This is known as "word of mouth." If people are talking about your podcast, you should attract new listeners.

Now that your podcast is online and listed on directories, it's time to spread the word. That means shouting about it!

Spreading the word

With many tens of thousands of podcasts to choose from, many of them made by famous and popular broadcasters or celebrities, it's hard for a new show to get noticed. To begin with, you may only attract a handful of listeners who stumble on your show while browsing podcast directories. If you want people to listen, you'll need to work hard on promotion.

You should start by getting people you know to listen to the show. Tell friends, family, and classmates about it, and ask them to tell people they know, too.

STAY SAFE

When using the Internet, always get a parent, teacher, or other responsible adult to help you. Don't talk to strangers on chat services, no matter how friendly they seem.

Tune in to a brand new podcast, all about life at Newfield Heights High!

The School Life Podcast

THE SCHOOL LIFE PODCAST

SUBSCRIBE TO OUR EPISODES TO HEAR:

> News from the school's clubs and sports teams

> Interviews with students and teachers

> What's hot and what's not around school

> Jokes and stories guaranteed to make you laugh!

Listen to the first episode on our web site, or find us on all good podcast directories!

www.theschoollifepodcast.com

Why not make some posters advertising your podcast and hang them up at school? This is your chance to create excitement about your podcast!

Get online

Since your podcast is online, use the Internet to promote it. Many podcasters use social networking sites such as Facebook and Twitter to promote their shows. You have to be at least 13 years of age to use these services, so you might have to get an adult to do it on your behalf. You could also ask other podcasters to be guests on your show, so they bring their listeners to your podcast. They may even ask you to appear on their podcasts to publicize yours.

CHAPTER 5

Developing Your
PODCAST

Once you have the hang of recording podcasts, you can start to be more adventurous. Recording spontaneous interviews, as many journalists do, is just one example of how you could develop your podcast.

Once you've made a handful of podcast episodes, it's a good idea to start focusing on where your series can go next. If you have the theme, format, and style of your podcast right, it should be able to run for a long time.

Popular movie podcast *Filmspotting* is a great example of this. Since movie fans Adam Kempenaar and Sam Van Hallgren launched it in 2005, the series has created over 500 episodes. In that time, the format has barely changed, but the podcast is as popular as ever.

Take your time

It's a good idea to let your podcast develop at its own pace. Record a number of episodes over a few months before you work hard to promote the series. During this time, you can try out different segments, improve your editing skills, practice interviewing guests, and get a handle on the best way to promote your show to listeners. Once you're happy with it, try releasing episodes on a more regular basis, either weekly or every other week.

Success Story

While he was in college, Jesse Thorn started his own weekly show called *The Sound of Young America*. It featured Jesse interviewing a guest, usually a young comedian. Over time, he renamed it *Bullseye* and turned it into a magazine-style show, with a number of interviews and segments. It's now broadcast on over 60 public radio stations throughout the United States.

You want listeners to enjoy your podcast so much that they eagerly await each new episode.

Building an audience

Releasing podcast episodes regularly is a good way to attract listeners, but how else can you build up a loyal audience? Unfortunately, there's no perfect recipe for winning fans, but there are lots of things you can try:

- Involve listeners by asking them to send in questions and ideas for topics to cover in future episodes.
- Invite enthusiastic fans to take part in panel discussions on episodes as a reward for their loyalty.
- Secure interviews with famous guests or experts on your subject.
- Get other popular podcasters to promote your podcast on social media or through their web sites, in exchange for you promoting theirs.

Looking at statistics

Another good way to see how your podcast is going is to look at the number of times each episode is downloaded or listened to. Many streaming web sites, such as SoundCloud and Mixcloud, provide this information, though sometimes you have to pay for it. But you can also think about what your most popular episodes have in common. If listeners frequently respond to a particular type of show or feature, try doing more of these.

Success Story

Answer Me This is a comedy podcast created every two weeks by Helen Zaltzman and Olly Mann, also starring Dr. Martin Austwick ("Martin the Sound Man"). Listeners send in questions on any subject and the team answers them. The podcast began in Zaltzman's living room in January 2007. It has since become one of the United Kingdom's most successful independently produced podcasts and has received many awards, including Sony Radio Academy Awards' Best Internet Program of 2011.

Did you know that some podcasters create video versions of their shows, known as vodcasts? You could try doing this. All you need is a smartphone, some video-editing software, and a few great ideas!

Video podcasting

If podcasts offer a chance to make your own radio show, then video podcasts, or vodcasts, allow you to make short TV shows. Vodcasts are generally not as popular as regular podcasts, but can help you reach different audiences.

If you secure a cool interview for your podcast, you could film it at the same time and turn the video footage into a vodcast. You could also record a special video edition of your podcast, introducing regular contributors to a whole new audience who use video-sharing sites. You'll have to upload any vodcasts you create to a video-sharing site, such as Vimeo or YouTube, rather than your usual podcast-hosting service.

STAY SAFE

If you're thinking of making a vodcast, always take a responsible adult with you when you go out filming. Remember that you have to be at least 13 years old to upload videos to YouTube or Vimeo. If you're younger than this, get an adult to do it for you.

Get vodcasting!

If you want to try your hand at making a vodcast, you'll need:

- something to film it on. This could be a smartphone, tablet computer, or camcorder.
- video-editing software. Popular free or cheap packages include Windows Movie Maker for PC and iMovie for Mac. Once you've filmed your vodcast, transfer the file to your computer for editing. Then, the process of getting it ready for uploading to the Internet begins.

The most popular vodcasts tend to be no longer than 10 minutes, so try to keep it succinct. If you have recorded a really good, but long, interview with someone, you can always split it into a number of parts. Most video editing software allows you to mix in music or sound effects. If your podcast has a theme song, or radio-style jingle, why not use that at the start?

Blogger Zoe Sugg (known as Zoella) became an Internet sensation after launching a weekly vodcast series in the year 2000. Her YouTube channel now has over nine million subscribers, and she's launched her own range of beauty products.

CONCLUSION

Just the Beginning!

Now that you know how to get your ideas, interests, and, most importantly, your voice online, your podcasting journey is ready to begin. This is the start of a podcasting voyage that could, in time, lead to a career in the media. Given that many people see podcasts as the future of radio, there's no better time to get started!

Podcasting teaches you many of the skills needed to host and produce radio shows, and could lead to a future career in professional broadcasting.

The future of radio

Statistics prove that more people than ever before are listening to podcasts. The percentage of Americans who have listened to a podcast in the last month almost doubled between 2008 and 2015, going from 9 percent to 17 percent. Three of the biggest public radio networks in the United States have launched their own podcast networks. Because of this, they're always looking for new podcasts that could, one day, also be broadcast on established radio stations.

A fun hobby

While a media career may be years away, podcasting is a great hobby to start you on the broadcasting path. No matter what your passion is, podcasting gives you the opportunity to be creative while learning and developing new skills. You should now have some great transferable skills, such as the ability to research and plan projects (very useful for schoolwork), plus some that are specific to broadcasting and journalism. If you become a dedicated podcaster, who knows where it may take you?

Glossary

angle particular way of presenting a subject

audience group of podcast listeners or people who have gathered in one place to watch a performance

broadcast distribute information, speech, and music to people through television, radio, or podcasting

DJ mix seamless musical performance created by a DJ

download transfer a computer file or files from the Internet to a computer or mobile device

downloadable any computer file that can be transferred from the Internet to a computer or mobile device

drama telling a story using actors

framework structure of your podcast, for which you decide what features you'll include and in what order. Each episode might use the same framework.

jingle short, catchy recording containing a mixture of speech and music, used in radio, podcasting, and advertising

mixing process of setting sound levels on a piece of music, radio show, or podcast

mixing desk professional piece of equipment used to adjust the sound levels on a piece of music, radio broadcast, or podcast

monologue talk or performance by a single person—for example, a broadcaster or comedian

MP3 file type of computer file used to distribute music and sound recordings over the Internet. MP3 files are popular due to their small size, making downloading them quick and easy.

multitracking method of sound recording where several recordings are layered up to create a finished song, radio show, or podcast
obscure not very well-known

panel discussion conversation between a number of people, usually organized and led by a host

public radio any radio station or service set up to entertain and inform a wide range of people, rather than make money as a business

record company business that specializes in marketing and distributing music

RSS feed file that attaches itself to a podcast and contains information on what the podcast is and where you can find it on the Internet

sound card piece of equipment used to connect microphones and musical instruments to a computer. Sound cards can either be built into a computer or an external piece of equipment plugged into a computer.

streaming sending or receiving music, audio, or video content over the Internet as a steady, continuous flow

subscriber person who commits to receiving a product, such as a podcast, magazine, or satellite television service, on a regular basis

theme subject or idea behind something—for example, a podcast's theme could be baking

track sound recording

upload transfer a computer file from your computer or mobile device to a remote storage computer, known as a server, using the Internet

USB system for connecting a wide range of devices (microphones, printers, hard drives, sound cards, phones, digital cameras, and so on) into a computer

vodcast short for "video podcast"

Find Out More

Books

Anniss, Matt. *Make a Podcast* (Find Your Talent). Mankato, Minn.: Arcturus, 2012.

Fontichiaro, Kristin. *Speak Out: Making Podcasts and Other Audio Recordings* (Information Explorer Junior). Ann Arbor: Cherry Lake, 2013.

Fontichiaro, Kristin. *Super Smart Information Strategies: Podcasting 101.* Ann Arbor: Cherry Lake, 2011.

Web sites

Free Music Archive
www.freemusicarchive.org
This excellent web site contains lots of great music that you can use, free of charge, in your podcasts. All the music has been donated by creators, and it covers every style you can think of.

The Free Sound Project
www.freesound.org
This is a great place to find sound effects and bursts of music for your podcasts, completely free of charge! If you're feeling generous, you could even record music of your own and add it to the web site for other users to download.

Jake Ludington's Digital Lifestyle: Recording a Podcast
www.jakeludington.com/podcasting/20050222_recording_a_podcast. html
Read this simple step-by-step guide to recording a podcast using the free software program Audacity. You'll see how easy it can be.

Podfeed: Kids and Teens
www.podfeed.net/category/7/Kids+and+Teens
If you're having trouble finding inspiration, check out some of the other podcasts created by young people listed on this popular directory.

Further research

If you're more interested in the production side of podcasting—sound recording, mixing, and so on—then you might benefit from taking a sound production class. Many charities and not-for-profit organizations offer sound engineering and production classes for young people. There may even be one in your area.

If you're having trouble thinking of ideas for what your podcasts should be about, start by creating one for a school project. The fact that podcasts can be about anything means that you could do one for almost any subject. You could interview experts about your favorite period in history, tell the story of an inspirational scientist, write and perform your own stories and poems for English class, or even create a podcast for your geography class about a part of the world you've visited.

Finally, if you're hooked on podcasting and think a career in broadcasting or the media might be something to pursue in the future, take a trip to your local library. It should have books and other resources about what you'll need to do to become a journalist or radio host. You could even write to your local radio or TV station and ask for advice. Sometimes stations offer short internships for young people or visits to see how the station operates. The media are a competitive business, so the sooner you can get experience of that environment, the better.

Index